Not Just Socks

for kids

Sandi Rosner

Editorial Director   David Codling

Editor and Graphic Design   Gregory Courtney

Photography   Kathryn Martin

Photo Editing and Effects   Eric Youngquist

Clothing Stylist   Betsy Westman

Models   Aiden Braccia, Julianna Martin, Martin Schuler, Sofia Schuler, Katie Tong, and Frances Wentker

Color Reproduction and Printing   Regent Publishing Services

Published and Distributed By   Unicorn Books and Crafts, Inc.

Printed in China

ISBN   1-893063-20-8

1 2 3 4 5 6 7 8 9 10

Introduction

Self-striping sock yarns are perfect for kid's knits. Playful color combinations and lively stripe styles make charming children's garments. Fancy knitting is not required—the yarn will do the work for you. Best of all, unlike multicolored knits using conventional methods, there are few ends to weave in!

The fine gauge of sock yarn makes lightweight, supple knits that are in scale with small bodies. Because the pieces are small, there is no need to be intimidated by the small gauge. An adult sweater at this gauge might take a long time to knit, but a child's sweater is a manageable project.

This book uses both basic and more advanced techniques to make the most of the color changes in self-striping yarn. Some projects are within reach of all but the newest of beginners, while others will challenge the skills of an intermediate knitter. Please refer to a good knitting reference book if you find techniques that are new to you. There are many good "how to knit" books on the market, and no knitter's library is complete without at least one.

Have fun playing with different stripe styles. Take your little ones to the yarn store and let them choose their favorite colors. These projects are as fun to knit as they will be to wear.

Thoughts on Working with Self-striping Sock Yarns

〰 You don't have to use the colors in your yarn in the order they appear. Feel free to manipulate the color placement to please yourself. If you want green thumbs on your mittens, just wind off some yarn until you get to the green section. If you want your ribbed edges in a solid color, just wind off the spotted part.

〰 Pay attention to the sequence of colors in your yarn. If you want the pieces of a pair to match, you will want to make sure the colors appear in the same order. When you start a new ball of yarn, make sure the colors run in the same direction. Rarely, but sometimes, the sequence will reverse from skein to skein, even within the same dye lot. You may need to work one skein from the outside and the next from the inside strand in order to keep the sequence consistent.

〰 Some people love the look of an unmatched pair. For others, it just makes them crazy. You know who you are. If you want your pair to match, start the first piece at the junction between two colors. Wind off yarn to get to the same place in the color sequence when you start the second piece. If an unmatched look is more your style, just start wherever you are and let the colors fall as they may. Both approaches are reflected in the projects in this book.

〰 Remember that tiny changes in tension will affect how the colors in your yarn line up, particularly in the spotted sections. The spots may stack in one stripe, and form chevrons in another. Don't make yourself nuts trying to control this. Embrace serendipity! Allow your project to delight you with its idiosyncrasies.

〰 Stripe styles and colorways change each season, with some being discontinued to make room for new favorites. If you can't find the exact yarn used in the book, choose your favorite colors from the selection at your local yarn store. The length of the color stretches and proportion of solid color to speckles will affect the look of your project. The staff in your yarn shop should be able to tell you how a particular ball of yarn will work up so you can make a choice that will please you.

Hats

Hats

Hats

Hats

Hats

Hats

DIFFICULTY EASY

YARN LANA GROSSA MEILENWEIT MAGICO (100 (100, 100) GRAMS)

NEEDLES 16" CIRCULAR AND SET OF FOUR DOUBLE-POINTED US 2 (2.75 MM) *OR THE SIZE YOU NEED TO GET GAUGE*

SIZES BABY (TODDLER, BIG KID)
MEASUREMENTS 16" (18", 20") CIRCUMFERENCE

GAUGE 30 STS AND 40 ROWS = 4" IN STOCKINETTE STITCH

Swirly Hat

The delicate eyelet pattern and picot edge give this hat a feminine touch.

Eyelet Swirl Pattern

Round 1: * K7, K2tog, yo, repeat from * to end of round.
Rounds 2, 4, 6, 8, 10, 12, 14 &16: K.
Round 3: * K6, K2tog, yo, K1, repeat from * to end of round.
Round 5: * K5, K2tog, yo, K2, repeat from * to end of round.
Round 7: * K4, K2tog, yo, K3, repeat from * to end of round.
Round 9: * K3, K2tog, yo, K4, repeat from * to end of round.
Round 11: * K2, K2tog, yo, K5, repeat from * to end of round.
Round 13: * K1, K2tog, yo, K6, repeat from * to end of round.
Round 15: * K2tog, yo, K7, repeat from * to end of round. At end of round 15, move marker 1 st to the right.

Repeat Rounds 1-16.

Hat

Using circular needle, CO 117 (135, 153) sts. Join into a circle, being careful not to twist your stitches. Place marker to indicate beginning of round. Work 10 rounds in st st.

Next round (turning round): * K1, K2tog, yo, repeat from * to end of round.

Work 11 rounds in st st. Work Eyelet Swirl Pattern until piece measures approx. 6" from turning round, ending with round 16 of pattern.

Shape Crown

Change to double-pointed needles when necessary.
Round 1: * K7, K2tog, yo, repeat from * to end of round.
Round 2: * K6, K2tog, K1, repeat from * to end of round.
Round 3: * K5, K2tog, yo, K1, repeat from * to end of round.
Round 4: * K4, K2tog, K2, repeat from * to end of round.
Round 5: * K3, K2tog, yo, K2, repeat from * to end of round.
Round 6: * K2, K2tog, K3, repeat from * to end of round.
Round 7: * K1, K2tog, yo, K3, repeat from * to end of round.
Round 8: * K2tog, K4, repeat from * to last st, K1, move marker 1 st to the left.
Round 9: * K3, K2tog, yo, repeat from * to end of round.
Round 10: * K2, K2tog, K1, repeat from * to end of round.
Round 11: * K1, K2tog, yo, K1, repeat from * to end of round.
Round 12: * K2tog, K2, repeat from * to last st, K1, move marker 1 st to the left.
Round 13: * K1, K2tog, yo, repeat from * to end of round.
Round 14: * K2tog, K1, repeat from * to last st, K1, move marker 1 st to the left.
Round 15: * K2tog, yo, repeat from * to end of round.
Round 16: K2tog 13 (15, 17) times.
Round 17: K2tog 5 (6, 7) times, K3tog.

Break yarn, draw through remaining 6 (7, 8) sts, pull tight and fasten off. Weave in ends.

Wormy Hat

Change the look of this playful hat by varying the length of the "worms" or by making lots more. You could even cover the entire hat with "worms" and call it a funky wig!

DIFFICULTY EASY

YARN LANA GROSSA MEILENWEIT FANTASY (100 (100, 100) GRAMS)

NEEDLES 16" CIRCULAR AND SET OF FOUR DOUBLE-POINTED US 2 (2.75 MM) *OR THE SIZE YOU NEED TO GET GAUGE*

SIZES BABY (TODDLER, BIG KID)
MEASUREMENTS 16" (18", 20") CIRCUMFERENCE

GAUGE 30 STS AND 40 ROWS = 4" IN STOCKINETTE STITCH

K2 P2 Ribbing
Every round: * K2, P2, repeat from * to end of round.

Hat
Using circular needle, CO 120 (136, 152) sts. Join into a circle, being careful not to twist your stitches. Work in K2 P2 Ribbing until piece measures 2" from beg. Change to st st and work until piece measures 5" (6", 7") from beg.

Shape Crown
Set up round: * K15 (17, 19), pm, repeat from * to end of round—8 markers.

Next round (dec round): * K to 2 sts before marker, K2tog, repeat from * to end of round.

Next round: K.

Repeat last two rounds, changing to double-pointed needles when necessary, until 8 sts remain. Break yarn, draw through remaining 8 sts, pull tight and fasten off.

Knitted Cord
Using double-pointed needle, CO 3 sts. * Do not turn work. Push sts to other end of needle, draw yarn across back, and K3. Repeat from * until cord is desired length. Break yarn, draw through all sts and fasten off.

Make lengths of knitted cord as desired for "worms." The pictured hat shows 18 worms in lengths ranging from 3" to 5".

Finishing
Weave in ends. Sew worms to crown of hat. Block to finished measurements.

Elfin Hat

Note

*Use the Cable Cast-On Method throughout as follows, working entire instruction for initial cast-on, then working instructions between *'s for subsequent cast-ons.*

Make a slip knot and place on left-hand needle. Insert right-hand needle through loop as if to knit, wrap yarn around right-hand needle and pull loop through, twist, and place on left-hand needle. * Insert right-hand needle between 1st and 2nd sts on left-hand needle, wrap yarn around right-hand needle and pull loop through, twist, and place on left-hand needle; rep from *.

K3 P1 Ribbing

Row 1 (WS): K1, * P3, K1, repeat from *.
Row 2 (RS): P1, * K3, P1, repeat from *.

Repeat Rows 1-2.

Hat

Using circular needle, CO 53 (65, 77) sts. Work in K3 P1 Ribbing for 2 rows, then maintaining ribbing as established, CO 2 sts at beg of next 8 rows—69 (81, 93) sts. Work 6 rows without shaping, then CO 2 sts at beg of next 4 rows—77 (89, 101) sts. CO 31 sts—108 (120, 132) sts. Place marker to indicate beg of round. Join, being careful not to twist your sts and continue in ribbing as established until piece measures 5½" (6", 6½") at longest section.

Shape Crown

Change to double-pointed needles when necessary.

Set-up round: * work 12 sts in ribbing, pm, repeat from * to end of round—9 (10, 11) markers.

Next round (dec round): * work in ribbing to 2 sts before marker, K2tog, repeat from * to end of round.

K the knit sts and P the purl sts, working dec round every 4th round until 9 (10, 11) sts remain. K 3 more rounds.

Last round: K2tog 3 (5, 4) times, K3tog 1 (0, 1) time. Break yarn, draw through remaining 4 (5, 5) sts, pull tight and fasten off.

Corkscrew Tassels (Make 3)

CO 20 sts. (K1, yo, K1) in each st. BO. Use tails to sew corkscrews to point of hat. Weave in ends.

Cozy and cute, this hat will keep little ears warm.

Dress Up

Dress Up

Dress Up

Dress Up

Dress Up

Dress Up

Dress Up

Back

With smaller needles, CO 86 (90, 98, 102) sts.

Row 1 (WS): P2, * K2, P2, repeat from * to end of row.
Row 2 (RS): K2, * P2, K2, repeat from * to end of row.

Repeat these two rows until piece measures 1½", ending with a WS row. Change to larger needle.

Next row (RS): K14 (16, 20, 22), * P2, work row 1 of Cable Chart, P2, K6, repeat from * twice more, P2, work row 1 of Cable Chart, P2, K14 (16, 20, 22).

Work in pattern as established, with st st at each side and between cables, until piece measures 7½" (8½", 10½", 12") from beg, ending with a WS row.

Shape Armholes

Maintaining pattern as established, BO 5 sts at beg of next 2 rows, then BO 4 sts at beg of following 2 rows. Dec 1 st at beg and end of every RS row twice—64 (68, 76, 80) sts. ◆◆

Work even in pattern until armhole measures 5" (6", 7", 7½"), ending with a WS row.

Shape Shoulders

BO 6 (6, 6, 7) sts at beg of next 2 rows, BO 6 (5, 6, 7) sts at beg of next 2 rows, then BO 5 (5, 6, 6) sts at beg of next 2 rows. Place remaining 30 (36, 40, 40) sts on a stitch holder.

Front

Work same as for back to ◆◆.

Shape Front Neck

Work 32 (34, 38, 40) sts in pattern. Place remaining sts on a stitch holder. Continue as set on left front only, **AND AT SAME TIME**, dec 1 st at neck edge every RS row 15 (18, 20, 20) times. Work even until same length as back to shoulders. BO 6 (6, 6, 7) sts at beg of next RS row, BO 6 (5, 6, 7) sts at beg of next RS row, then BO remaining 5 (5, 6, 6) sts. Return held sts

DIFFICULTY INTERMEDIATE

YARN LANA GROSSA MEILENWEIT MEGA BOOTS STRETCH (100 (100, 200, 200) GRAMS)

NEEDLES 16" CIRCULAR US 2 (2.75 MM) AND STRAIGHT OR CIRCULAR US 3 (3.25 MM) *OR THE SIZE YOU NEED TO GET GAUGE*

SIZES 2-4 (4-6, 6-8, 8-10)
CHEST 26" (28", 30", 32")
LENGTH 13" (15", 18", 20")

GAUGE 26 STS AND 36 ROWS = 4" IN STOCKINETTE STITCH ON US 3

Cabled Vest

Knitted in a yarn designed to make broad stripes, this vest can turn pants and a polo shirt into a dressed-up outfit he'll be happy to wear.

The classic design works just as well for preppy girls.

to needle, reattach yarn, and complete the RS row. Work 1 WS row. Dec 1 st at neck edge every RS row 15 (18, 20, 20) times. Work even until same length as back to shoulders. BO 6 (6, 6, 7) sts at beg of next WS row, BO 6 (5, 6, 7) sts at beg of next WS row, then BO remaining 5 (5, 6, 6) sts.

Finishing
Sew back to front at shoulders.

Neckband
Move back neck sts from holder to smaller 16" circular needle. Attach yarn at right shoulder and work back neck sts as follows: *K2, P2, repeat from *; pick up and knit 36 (40, 48, 52) sts down left front neck, pm, pick up and knit 36 (40, 48, 52) sts up right front neck—102 (116, 136, 144) sts. Join into a circle, being careful not to twist your sts, and work in the round as follows:

Round 1: Work in K2, P2 ribbing as set to 1 st before marker, K1, sl marker, K1, continue in K2, P2 ribbing to end.

Round 2: Work in ribbing as set to 2 sts before marker, K2tog, sl marker, SSK, continue in ribbing as set to end.

Repeat these 2 rounds 3 times more. BO in pattern.

Armbands
With smaller 16" circular needle, pick up and knit 88 (96, 112, 120) sts along armhole edge and work in rows as follows.

Next 6 rows: *K2, P2, repeat from * to end of row.

BO in pattern. Sew side seams (including armbands). Weave in ends. Block to finished measurements.

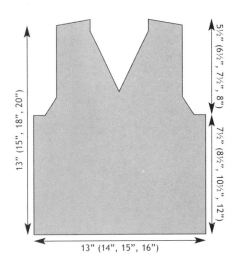

Cable Chart

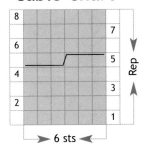

6 sts

K on right side rows; P on wrong side rows.

sl 3 sts to cn and hold at back; K3; K3 from cn.

Cape

Cable Cast-On Method
* Insert right-hand needle between 1st and 2nd sts on left-hand needle, wrap yarn around right-hand needle and pull loop through, twist, and place on left-hand needle; rep from *.

Special Abbreviation
MB—Make Bobble: (K1, P1, K1, P1, K1) all in same st— 5 sts. (Turn, sl 1, K4) 4 times, turn, pass 2nd, 3rd, 4th and 5th sts over 1st st.

Right Back
With larger needles, CO 48 (52, 56, 61) sts. Work in st st, **AND AT SAME TIME**, dec 1 st at beg of every 6th (6th, 6th, 8th) row 9 (10, 10, 9) times—39 (42, 46, 52) sts, then dec 1 st at beg of every RS row 25 (28, 30, 33) times. BO remaining 14 (14, 16, 19) sts.

Left Back
With larger needles, CO 48 (52, 56, 61) sts. Work in st st, **AND AT SAME TIME**, dec 1 st at end of every 6th (6th, 6th, 8th) row 9 (10, 10, 9) times—39 (42, 46, 52) sts, then dec 1 st at end of every RS row 25 (28, 30, 33) times. BO remaining 14 (14, 16, 19) sts.

Left Front
Work as for right back until 18 (18, 20, 23) sts remain. BO 6 (6, 8, 11) sts at beg of next WS row. Dec 1 st at beg and end of every RS row 4 times. BO remaining 4 sts.

Right Front
Work as for left back until 19 (19, 21, 24) sts remain. BO 6 (6, 8, 11) sts at beg of next RS row, then dec 1 st at end of row. Dec 1 st at beg and end of every RS row 4 times. BO remaining 4 sts.

Sides (Make 2)
With larger needles, CO 74 (82, 86, 90) sts. Work in st st, **AND AT SAME TIME**, dec 1 st at beg and end of every 6th (6th, 6th, 8th) row 9 (10, 10, 9) times—56 (62, 66, 72) sts, then dec 1 st at beg and end of every RS row 25 (28, 30, 33) times. BO remaining 6 sts.

Assembly
With larger needle, using speckled sections of yarn, pick up and knit 78 (87, 90, 103) sts along shaped side of right front panel. With second needle, pick up and knit 78 (87, 90, 103) sts along corresponding side of side panel. With WS's together, join using 3-needle bind off method. Repeat to join each panel, leaving front open.

Lower Border

With smaller needle, using non-speckled sections of yarn, with RS facing and beg at left front, pick up and knit 336 (372, 396, 420) sts along lower edge. Use Cable Cast-On Method to cast on 6 more sts.

Row 1 (WS): Sl 1, K4, K2tog (last st of border with 1 st picked up from edge).
Row 2 (RS): Sl 1, K2, yo, K3.
Row 3 (and all WS rows): Sl 1, K to last st, K2tog.
Row 4: Sl 1, K2, yo, K4.
Row 6: Sl 1, K2, yo, K5.
Row 8: Sl 1, K2, yo, K6.
Row 10: Sl 1, K2, yo, K7.
Row 12: Sl 1, K2, yo, K7, MB.
Row 13: BO 6 sts, K to last st, K2tog.

Repeat rows 2-13 until all picked up sts have been used. BO.

Neckband

With smaller needle, using non-specked sections of yarn, with RS facing, pick up and knit 14 (16, 18, 20) sts along right front, 1 st at seam, 5 sts along top of right side, 1 st at seam, 12 (14, 16, 18) sts along right back, 1 st at seam, 12 (14, 16, 18) sts along left back, 1 st at seam, 5 sts along top of left side, 1 st at seam, and 14 (16, 18, 20) sts along left front—71 (75, 83, 93) sts. Work 7 rows in garter st. BO loosely.

Button Band

With smaller needle, using non-specked sections of yarn, with RS facing, pick up and knit 4 sts down left end of neckband, 78 (87, 90, 103) sts along left front edge, and 4 sts at top section of lower border, leaving point free—86 (95, 98, 111) sts. Work 11 rows in garter st. BO.

Buttonhole Band

With smaller needle, using non-speckled sections of yarn, with RS facing, pick up and knit 4 sts at top section of lower border, leaving point free, 78 (87, 90, 103) sts along right front edge, and 4 sts at right end of neckband—86 (95, 98, 111) sts. Work 6 rows in garter st.

Row 7 (buttonhole row): K3, K2tog, yo, (K12, K2tog, yo) twice, K to end of row.

Work 4 rows in garter st. BO.

Finishing

Sew buttons opposite buttonholes. Weave in ends and block to finished measurements.

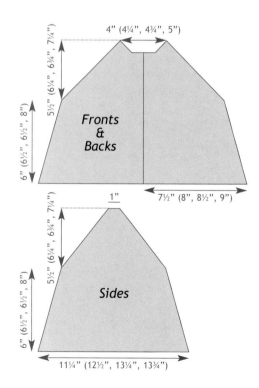

Every little girl will feel like a fairy princess in this pretty cape.

DIFFICULTY INTERMEDIATE

YARN LANA GROSSA MEILENWEIT MULTIRINGEL (200 (200, 200, 300) GRAMS)

NEEDLES 16" CIRCULAR US 2 (2.75 MM) AND STRAIGHT OR CIRCULAR US 3 (3.25 MM) *OR THE SIZE YOU NEED TO GET GAUGE*

SIZES 2-4 (4-6, 6-8, 8-10)

WAIST 21" (22", 24", 25")
LENGTH 21" (24", 28", 32")

GAUGE 26 STS AND 32 ROWS = 4" IN STOCKINETTE STITCH ON US 3

Girl's Jumper

Note
Knit the skirt section sideways in one piece, shaping with short rows. Pick up sts along the top of the skirt and work the bodice.

Skirt
With larger needles and waste yarn, CO 78 (90, 104, 118) sts. Change to main yarn.

Row 1 (RS): Sl 1, (K1, P1) 5 times, K to end of row.
Row 2 (WS): Sl 1, P to last 12 sts, (K1, P1) 5 times, end with K2.

Repeat these two rows 3 times more.

Row 9 (RS): Sl 1, (K1, P1) 5 times, K57 (69, 83, 97), W&T, P to last 12 sts, (K1, P1) 5 times, K2, turn, sl 1, (K1, P1) 5 times, K41 (53, 67, 81), W&T, P to last 12 sts, (K1, P1) 5 times, K2, turn, sl 1, (K1, P1) 5 times, K25 (37, 51, 65), W&T, P to last 12 sts, (K1, P1) 5 times, K2, turn, sl 1, (K1, P1) 5 times, K to end of row, picking up the wraps as you come to them—6 short rows worked.

Row 10 (WS): Sl 1, P to last 12 sts, (K1, P1) 5 times, end with K2.

Work these 10 rows 17 (18, 19, 20) times.

Remove waste yarn. As you pick out the waste yarn stitch-by-stitch, you will free the bottom loops of your first row of knitting. Place these new stitches on your smaller needle. Graft the ends of skirt together using the kitchener stitch.

Bodice
With smaller needle, RS facing, pick up and knit 126 (134, 142, 150) sts along narrow end of skirt (approx. 3 sts for every 4 rows). Place marker for beg of round and work in seed stitch as follows:

Next round: K1, P1, rep from * to end of round.
Next round: P1, K1, rep from * to end of round.

Rep these 2 rounds for 1".

Divide for Front and Back
Change to larger needle.

Next row (RS): BO 10 sts, sl 1 (K1, P1) 3 times, K39 (43, 47, 51), (P1, K1) 3 times, K1, place these 53 (57, 61, 65) sts on a holder for front. BO 10 sts, sl 1 (K1, P1) 3 times, K39 (43, 47, 51) sts, (P1, K1) 3 times, K1. Continue working on these 53 (57, 61, 65) sts for back, with seed stitch at sides, and st st in center, until work measures 7" (8", 10", 12") from pick up, ending with RS facing for next row.

*This
jumper
is an
easy-to-wear
option for
school
or play.*

Shape Back Neck

Next row (RS): Work 14 sts in pattern, place remaining 39 (43, 47, 51) sts on a holder.

Maintaining st st and seed stitch as established, BO 3 sts at beg of next WS row, then 2 sts at beg of next WS row, then 1 st at beg of next WS row. Continue in seed stitch on remaining 8 sts until work measures 9" (10", 12", 14") from pick up. BO. Return held sts to needle and rejoin yarn.

Next Row (RS): BO 25 (29, 33, 37) sts, work in established patterns to end of row.

BO 3 sts at beg of next RS row, then 2 sts at beg of next RS row, then 1 st at beg of next RS row. Continue in seed stitch on remaining 8 sts until 9" (10", 14") from pick up. BO.

Front

Return front sts to needle and reattach yarn. Work as for back until work measures 5" (6", 8", 10") from pick up, ending with RS facing for next row.

Next row (RS): Work 17 sts in pattern, place remaining 36 (40, 44, 48) sts on a holder.

Maintaining st st and seed st as established, BO 3 sts at beg of next WS row, then 2 sts at beg of next WS row, then 1 st at beg of next 4 WS rows. Continue in seed st on remaining 8 sts until same length as back to shoulders. BO. Return held sts to needle and rejoin yarn.

Next Row (RS): BO 19 (23, 27, 31) sts, work in established patterns to end of row.

BO 3 sts at beg of next RS row, then 2 sts at beg of next RS row, then 1 st at beg of next 4 RS rows. Continue in seed st on remaining 8 sts until same length as back to shoulders. BO. Sew front to back at shoulders.

Neckband

With smaller needle, RS facing, beg at right shoulder seam, pick up and knit 16 sts down right back neck, 25 (29, 33, 37) sts across back neck, 16 sts up left back neck, 27 sts down left front neck, 19 (23, 27, 31) sts across front neck, and 27 sts up right front neck—130 (138, 146, 154) sts. Join and work in the round as follows:

Round 1: * K1, P1, repeat from * to end of round.
Round 2: * P1, K1, repeat from * to end of round.

Repeat these 2 rounds until neckband measures 1". BO.

Finishing

Weave in ends. Block to finished measurements.

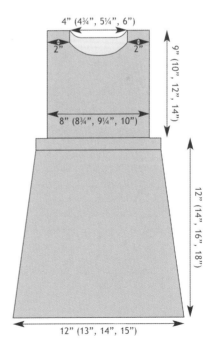

Mittens

Mittens

Mittens

Mittens

Mittens

Mittens

Mittens

*The frill
on the
cuff adds
a little fun
to these
classic
hand
warmers.*

Cuff

CO 126 (132, 144) sts. Divide stitches evenly on three needles and join into a circle, being careful not to twist your stitches.

Rounds 1-10: * K3, P3, repeat from * to end of round.

Next round: *K3tog, P3tog, repeat from * to end of round—42 (44, 48) sts.

Next round: * K1, P1, repeat from * to end of round.

Repeat this round for 1½". Change to st st and K one round.

Palm

Set up round: K21 (22, 24), pm, m1, pm, K21 (22, 24).

Increase round: K to marker, sl marker, m1, K to marker, m1, sl marker, K to end of round.

Continue in st st, working increase round every 3rd round 6 times more—15 sts between markers—57 (59, 63) sts total.

Next round: K to marker, remove marker, place gusset sts on waste yarn for holding, remove marker, CO 1 st to bridge the gap, K to end of round—43 (45, 49) sts.

Work even until palm measures 3½" (4", 4½") above ribbing, dec'g 3 (1, 1) st on last row—40 (44, 48) sts.

Shape Top

Set up round: * K10 (11, 12), pm, repeat from * 3 times more.

Next round (dec round): * K to 2 sts before marker, K2tog, sl marker, repeat from * 3 times more.

Continue in st st, working dec round every other round 2 (3, 4) times, then every round 7 times—4 sts remain. Break yarn, draw through remaining sts, pull tight and fasten off.

DIFFICULTY INTERMEDIATE

YARN LANA GROSSA MEILENWEIT COLORTWEED (100 (100, 100) GRAMS)

NEEDLES SET OF 4 DOUBLE-POINTED US 2 (2.75 MM) *OR THE SIZE YOU NEED TO GET GAUGE*

SIZES 4-6 (6-8, 8-12)
MEASUREMENTS 6" (6½", 7") HAND CIRCUMFERENCE AROUND PALM ABOVE THUMB

GAUGE 28 STS AND 44 ROWS = 4" IN STOCKINETTE STITCH

Ruffled Mittens

Thumb

Place held gusset sts on needles. Join yarn and pick up 1 st at palm—16 sts. Arrange sts evenly on 3 needles and work until thumb measures 1" (1¼", 1¼").

Next round: * K2, K2tog, repeat from * 3 times more.
Next round: K.
Next round: * K1, K2tog, repeat from * 3 times more.

Last round: K2tog 4 times. Break yarn and draw through remaining 4 sts. Pull tight and fasten off.

Weave in ends, using ends to close up any gaps at base of thumb. Block to finished measurements.

DIFFICULTY INTERMEDIATE

YARN LANA GROSSA MEILENWEIT MEETING
(100 (100, 100) GRAMS)

NEEDLES SET OF FOUR DOUBLE-POINTED US 2 (2.75 MM) *OR THE SIZE YOU NEED TO GET GAUGE*

SIZES 4-6 (6-8, 8-12)
MEASUREMENTS 6" (6½", 7") HAND CIRCUMFERENCE AROUND PALM ABOVE THUMB

GAUGE 28 STS AND 44 ROWS = 4" IN STOCKINETTE STITCH

X-Ribbed Mittens

These cozy mittens have the added detail of a crossed rib pattern on the cuff.

K2 P2 Ribbing
Every Round: * K2, P2, repeat from * to end of round.

Cuff
Loosely CO 40 (48, 48) sts. Divide stitches evenly on three needles and join into a circle, being careful not to twist your stitches. Work in K2 P2 Ribbing for 5 rounds. Work the 9 rounds of Chart. Work in K2 P2 Ribbing for 5 rounds.

Next round—
First size only: K10, m1, K20, m1, K10—42 sts.
Second size only: * K10, K2tog, repeat from * 3 times more—44 sts.
Third size only: K—48 sts.

Palm
Set-up round: K21 (22, 24), pm, m1, pm, K21 (22, 24).

Next round (inc round): K to marker, sl marker, m1, K to marker, m1, sl marker, K to end of round.

Continue in st st, working increase round every 3rd round 6 times more—15 sts between markers—57 (59, 63) sts total.

Next round: K to marker, remove marker, place gusset stitches on waste yarn for holding, remove marker, CO 1 st to bridge the gap, K to end of round—43 (45, 49) sts.

Work even until palm measures 3½" (4", 4½") above ribbing, dec'g 3 (1, 1) st(s) evenly on last row—40 (44, 48) sts.

Shape Top
Set up round: * K10 (11, 12), pm, repeat from * 3 times more.

Next round (dec round): * K to 2 sts before marker, K2tog, sl marker, repeat from * 3 times more.
Continue in st st, working dec round every other round 2 (3, 4) times, then every round 7 times—4 sts remain.

Break yarn, draw through remaining sts, pull tight and fasten off.

Thumb
Place held gusset sts on needles. Join yarn and pick up 1 st at palm—16 sts. Arrange sts evenly on 3 needles and work until thumb measures 1" (1¼", 1¼").

Next round: * K2, K2tog, repeat from * 3 times more.
Next round: K.
Next round: * K1, K2tog, repeat from * 3 times more.
Last round: K2tog 4 times.

Break yarn and draw through remaining 4 sts. Pull tight and fasten off.

Finishing
Weave in ends, using ends to close up any gaps at base of thumb. Block to finished measurements.

Cable Chart

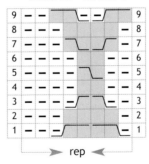

rep

▨	K.
−	P.
	sl 1 st to cn and hold at front; K1; K1 from cn.
	sl 1 st to cn and hold at back; K1; K1 from cn.
	sl 1 st to cn and hold at front; P1; K1 from cn.
	sl 1 st to cn and hold at back; K1; P1 from cn.
	sl 2 sts to cn and hold at front; P1; K2 from cn.
	sl 1 st to cn and hold at back; K2; P1 from cn.

Play

Play

Play

Play

Play

Play

Hooded Pullover

This lightweight layer sports a classic hood and kangaroo pocket.

Cable Cast-On Method

* Insert right-hand needle between 1st and 2nd sts on left-hand needle, wrap yarn around right-hand needle and pull loop through, twist, and place on left-hand needle; rep from *.

Back

With smaller needles, CO 82 (90, 98, 102) sts.

Row 1 (WS): P2, * K2, P2, repeat from * to end of row.
Row 2 (RS): K2, * P2, K2, repeat from * to end of row.

Repeat these two rows until piece measures 1½", ending with a WS row. Change to larger needles and work in st st, inc'g 3 (1, 1, 3) sts evenly across first row—85 (91, 99, 105) sts. Work even in st st until piece measures 8½" (9½", 11", 12½") from beg, ending with a WS row.

Shape Raglan

BO 5 sts at beg of next 2 rows.

Dec as follows every 4th row 0 (3, 0, 2) times, then every other row 24 (23, 29, 29) times:

Decrease row: K2, SSK, K to last 4 sts, K2tog, K2.

BO rem 27 (29, 31, 33) sts.

Front

Work same as for back through raglan shaping until 53 (55, 57, 59) sts remain, ending with a WS row.

Next row: K2, SSK, K25 (26, 27, 28). Place remaining 24 (25, 26, 27) sts on holder for right front.

Next row (WS): Sl 1, (P1, K1) twice, P to end of row.

Continue raglan shaping at armhole edge and maintain rib at neck edge until 21 (22, 23, 24) sts remain, ending with a WS row.

Next row (RS): K2, SSK, K5 (6, 7, 8), K2tog, K1. Place remaining 9 sts on holder for front neck.
Next row (WS): P.
Next row: K2, SSK, K to last 3 sts, K2tog, K1.

Repeat last 2 rows until 4 (5, 6, 7) sts remain. BO. Return right front sts to needle. Use Cable CO Method to CO 5 sts at beg of row (neck edge).

Next row (RS): Sl 1, (K1, P1) twice, K to last 4 sts, K2tog, K2.

Continue raglan shaping at armhole edge and maintain rib at neck edge until 21 (22, 23, 24) sts remain, ending with a WS row.

Next row (RS): Sl 1, (K1, P1) twice, K4, place these 9 sts on holder for front neck, K1, SSK, K5 (6, 7, 8), K2tog, K2.
Next row (WS): P.
Next row: K1, SSK, K to last 4 sts, K2tog, K2.

Repeat last 2 rows until 4 (5, 6, 7) sts remain. BO.

Sleeves
With smaller needle, CO 38 (42, 46, 50) sts.

Row 1 (WS): P2, * K2, P2, repeat from * to end of row.
Row 2 (RS): K2, * P2, K2, repeat from * to end of row.

Repeat these two rows until piece measures 1½", ending with a WS row.

Change to larger needles and work in st st, inc'g 1 st at beg and end of every 8th row 11 (12, 13, 12) times—60 (66, 72, 74) sts. Continue without further shaping until piece measures 11½" (12", 13½", 14½") from beg.

Shape Raglan
BO 5 sts at beg of next 2 rows.

Dec as follows every 4th row 2 (4, 2, 6) times, then every other row 20 (20, 24, 20) times:

Decrease row: K2, SSK, K to last 4 sts, K2tog, K2.

BO rem 6 (8, 10, 12) sts.

Pocket
With larger needles, CO 10 sts. Working in st st, use Cable Cast-On Method to CO 3 sts at the end of every RS row 8 (10, 12, 14) times—34 (40, 46, 52) sts. Work even until piece measures 7" (7½", 8", 8½") from beg along straight side. BO 3 sts at beg of every WS row 8 (10, 12, 14) times. BO remaining 10 sts.

Pocket Edging
With smaller needles, RS facing, pick up and knit 24 (30, 36, 42) sts along diagonal edge of pocket.

Next Row (WS): K2, P2, rep from *.
Next Row (RS): K the K sts and P the P sts as they face you.

Rep these 2 rows until edging measures 1". BO loosely. Repeat for other diagonal edge. Sew pocket to front of sweater, matching centers and placing long straight side of pocket just above ribbing, leaving ribbed edges of pocket free. Sew sleeves to front and back at raglans.

Hood
With larger needles, pick up and knit 4 (5, 6, 7) sts along BO edge of right front, 6 (8, 10, 12) sts along top of right sleeve, 27 (29, 31, 33) sts along back neck edge, 6 (8, 10, 12) sts along top of left sleeve, and 4 (5, 6, 7) sts along BO edge of left front—47 (55, 63, 71) sts. P 1 row.

Next row: K10 (13, 16, 19), * m1, K2, repeat from * 12 (13, 14, 15) times more, m1, K11 (14, 17, 20)—61 (70, 79, 88) sts.

Work 3 rows without shaping.

Next row: K11 (14, 17, 20), * m1, K3, repeat from * 12 (13, 14, 15) times more, m1, K11 (14, 17, 20)—75 (85, 95, 105) sts.

Work without shaping until hood measures 8" (8½", 9", 9"), ending with a RS row.

Next row: P37 (42, 47, 52), pm, P1, pm, P37 (42, 47, 52).
Next row (decrease row): K to 2 sts before marker, K2tog, sl marker, K1, sl marker, SSK, K to end of row.
Next row (WS): P.

Repeat these 2 rows 8 times more. On last WS row, remove markers and P2tog in middle of row—56 (66, 76, 86) sts. Sl 28 (33, 38, 43) sts to smaller needle. Fold hood in half, holding needles parallel with WS's together. Graft center top of hood with kitchener stitch.

Neckband

With smaller needle, beg at right front neck, K2, P1, K1, P1, K4 from holder, pick up and knit 7 sts along right neck edge, 64 (68, 72, 72) sts along right side of hood to center, 1 st at center of hood, 64 (68, 72, 72) sts along left side of hood, 7 sts along left neck edge, and K4, P1, K1, P1, K2 from holder at left front neck—161 (169, 177, 177) sts.

Row 1 (WS): Sl 1, * P1, K1, repeat from * to end of row.
Row 2: Sl 1, * K1, P1, repeat from * to last 2 sts, end with K2.
Row 3: Repeat row 1.
Row 4 (buttonhole row): Work as for row 2 to last 5 sts, yo, K2tog, P1, K2.

Repeat rows 1 and 2 twice more. BO loosely.

Finishing

Sew side and sleeve seams. Sew button to neckband opposite buttonhole. Weave in ends. Block to finished measurements.

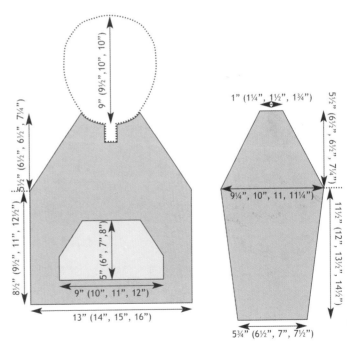

DIFFICULTY EASY

YARN LANA GROSSA MEILENWEIT MULTIEFFEKT (200 (200, 200) GRAMS)

NEEDLES 24" CIRCULAR US 2 (2.75 MM) AND STRAIGHT OR CIRCULAR US 3 (3.25 MM) *OR THE SIZE YOU NEED TO GET GAUGE*

SIZES 2-4 (4-6, 6-8)

CLOSED CHEST 24" (26", 28")
LENGTH 11" (12½", 13¼")
SLEEVE LENGTH (TO UNDERARM) 12" (13", 14")

GAUGE 26 STS AND 36 ROWS = 4" IN STOCKINETTE STITCH

Dancer's Wrap

She'll be the envy of all her friends in dance class when she wears this cute cardigan. Because it wraps around, it will grow as she does.

Notes
◆ Knit the body in one piece, starting at the end of the left side tie and working around the body to the end of the right side tie.
◆ Use Cable Cast-on Method (described below) when instructed to cast on at the end of a row.

Cable Cast-On Method
* Insert right-hand needle between 1st and 2nd sts on left-hand needle, wrap yarn around right-hand needle and pull loop through, twist, and place on left-hand needle; rep from *.

Body
With larger needles, CO 9 sts.

Every row: Sl 1, K to end of row.

Repeat this row (garter stitch with slip stitch selvedge) until piece measures 28" (30", 32").

Shape Left Front
Next row (RS): Sl 1, K8, CO 2.
Next row (WS): P2, pm, K9.
Next row: Sl 1, K to end of row, CO 2.
Next row: P to marker, K to end of row.

Repeat these last 2 rows 26 (30, 33) times more—65 (73, 79) sts. CO 7 sts at end of next RS row—72 (80, 86) sts. Work even in st st with garter st waistband for 2¾" (3", 3¼"), ending with a RS row.

Shape Left Armhole
◆ Next row (WS): BO 27 (29, 33) sts, work in pattern to end of row.
Next row (RS): Sl 1, K to end of row.
Next row (WS): BO 2, work in pattern to end of row.

Repeat these last 2 rows 2 times more—39 (45, 47) sts. Work 4 rows even.

Next row (RS): Sl 1, K to end of row, CO 2.
Next row (WS): P to marker, K to end of row.

Repeat these 2 rows 2 times more.

Next row (RS): Sl 1, K to end of row, CO 27 (29, 33) sts—72 (80, 86) sts. ◆ ◆

Back
Work even in st st with garter st waistband for 10" (11", 12"), ending with a RS row.

Shape Right Armhole
Repeat armhole shaping from ◆ to ◆ ◆. Work even in st st with garter st waistband for 2¾" (3", 3¼"), ending with a RS row.

Shape Right Front
Next row (WS): BO 7 sts.

Maintaining pattern as established, BO 2 sts at beg of every WS row 28 (32, 35) times—9 sts remain. Work in garter st with slip stitch selvedge until same length as left side tie.

Sleeves
With smaller needles, CO 39 (43, 45) sts.

Next row (WS): P1, * K1, P1, rep from * to end of row.
Next row (RS): K1, * P1, K1, rep from * to end of row.

Rep these 2 rows until ribbing measures 1½". Change to larger needles and work in st st, **AND AT SAME TIME**, inc 1 st at beg and end of every 6th row 11 (11, 12) times—61 (65, 69) sts. Continue without shaping until piece measures 12" (13", 14") from beg, ending with a WS row.

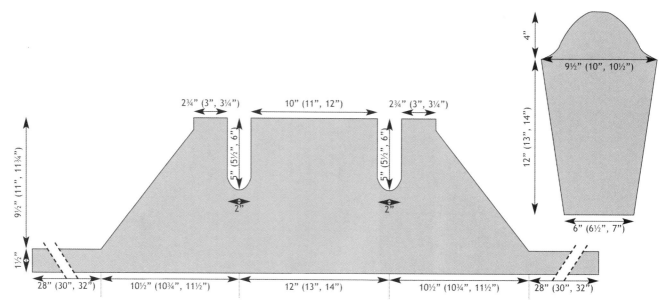

Shape Sleeve Cap

BO 3 sts at beg of next 2 rows, then dec 1 st at beg and end of every RS row 16 times—23 (27, 31) sts. BO 3 sts at beg of next 4 rows. BO rem 11 (15, 19) sts.

Finishing

Sew fronts to back at shoulders. Sew sleeve seams. Set sleeves into armholes and sew into place.

Neckband

With smaller needle, RS facing, pick up and knit 63 (71, 77) sts up right front neck edge, 30 (33, 36) sts along back neck, and 63 (71, 77) sts down left front neck edge—156 (175, 190) sts.

Next row (WS): * K1, P1, rep from *, end with K0 (1, 0).
Next row (RS): K the K sts and P the P sts as they face you.

Rep these 2 rows twice more, then work 1 more WS row. BO loosely in pattern. Sew ends of neckband to top of waistband. Weave in ends. Block to finished measurements.

Knit the matching leg warmers to complete the ensemble.

Leg Warmers

These leg warmers are an essential accessory for your budding ballerina or ice princess.

DIFFICULTY EASY

YARN LANA GROSSA MEILENWEIT MULTIEFFEKT (100) GRAMS)

NEEDLES SET OF 4 DOUBLE-POINTED US 2 (2.75 MM) *OR THE SIZE YOU NEED TO GET GAUGE*

SIZES TODDLER (BIG KID)

CIRCUMFERENCE 4½" (5½")
LENGTH 7" (10")

GAUGE 36 STS AND 40 ROWS = 4" IN K2 P2 RIBBING (SLIGHTLY STRETCHED)

K2 P2 Ribbing
Every round: * K2, P2, repeat from * to end of round.

Leg Warmers
Loosely CO 40 (48) sts. Arrange evenly on three needles and join into a circle, being careful not to twist your sts. Work in K2 P2 Ribbing until piece measures 7" (10"). BO loosely.

Finishing
Weave in ends. Leave unblocked as leg warmers will mold themselves to follow the shape of the wearer's leg.

Patchwork Pullover

Mitered squares join to form a bold graphic design on this pullover.

Notes

◆ The front and back of this sweater are each made up of 16 blocks. On the back, all blocks are the **Basic Block**. On the front, two of the blocks are the **Neck Block**. Knit the blocks separately and then sew them together. Pick up stitches for the sleeves, waistband and neckband.

◆ This design rewards careful placement of your colors. The bands and triangles of color made by the stripes in each block create larger squares and boxes when they meet the colors in adjoining blocks. In the sample shown, of the 30 basic blocks, 16 begin with the dark blue stripe; the remaining 14, plus the neck blocks, begin with the dark green stripe. To accomplish this, wind off yarn to get to the section you need. The yarn amounts specified allow plenty of yarn, so don't worry that you aren't using every little bit.

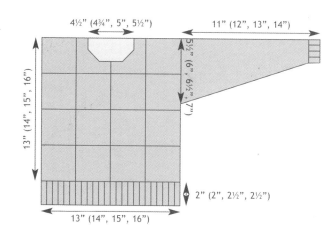

4½" (4¾", 5", 5½")   11" (12", 13", 14")

5½" (6", 6½", 7")

13" (14", 15", 16")

2" (2", 2½", 2½")

13" (14", 15", 16")

Basic Block (Make 30)

With larger needle, CO 41 (43, 47, 49) sts. Mark center st with a split stitch marker or safety pin.

Row 1 (WS): K.
Row 2 (and all RS rows): K to 1 st before center st, dbl dec, K to end.
Row 3: K.
Row 5: K.
Row 7: K.
Row 9: P.
Row 11: P.
Row 13: P.
Row 15: P.
Row 17 (and remaining WS rows): K.

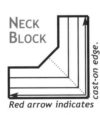

BASIC BLOCK

Red arrow indicates cast-on edge.

Continue as established until 3 sts remain. K3tog. Fasten off.

Neck Block (Make 2)

Work as for Basic Block above through row 11.
Row 12: BO 7 (8, 10, 11) sts (1 st remains on right-hand needle), K6, dbl dec, K to end.
Row 13: BO 7 (7, 10, 11) sts, P to end.
Row 14: SSK, K4, dbl dec, K4, K2tog.
Row 15: P.
Row 16: SSK, K2, dbl dec, K2, K2tog.
Row 17: P.
Row 18: SSK, dbl dec, K2tog.
Row 19: P3tog. Fasten off.

NECK BLOCK

Red arrow indicates cast-on edge.

Assembly

Sew blocks for back and front together as shown in diagrams on pages 54-55. Sew back to front at shoulders.

Sleeves

Place markers on sides of front and back 5½" (6", 6½", 7") down from shoulder seams. With larger needle, pick up and knit 70 (74, 80, 84) sts between markers. Work 4 (8, 8, 12) rows in st st. Continue in st st, dec'g 1 st at beg and end of every 4th row 18 (19, 21, 22) times—34 (36, 38, 40) sts, ending with a WS row. Change to smaller needles.

Next row (RS): * K2, P2, repeat from *, end K2 (0, 2, 0).
Next row (WS): P2 (0, 2, 0), * K2, P2, rep from * to end of row.

Rep these 2 rows until cuff measures 1½". BO loosely.

Waistband

With smaller needle, RS facing, pick up and knit 20 (21, 23, 24) sts for each block along lower edge—160 (168, 184, 192) sts. Place marker to indicate beg of round and work as follows:

Every round: * K2, P2, rep from * to end of row.

When waistband measures 2" (2", 2½", 2½"), BO loosely.

Neckband

With smaller needle, RS facing, beg at right shoulder seam, pick up and knit 30 (32, 36, 38) sts along back neck, 23 (24, 28, 31) sts down left side of neck to center front, and 23 (24, 28, 31) sts from center front up right side of neck—76 (80, 92, 100) sts. Place marker to indicate beg of round and work as follows:

Every round: * K2, P2, rep from * to end of round.

When neckband measures 1", BO loosely.

Finishing

Sew side and sleeve seams. Weave in ends. Block to finished measurements.

Back Assembly Diagram

Red arrow indicates cast-on edge for each block.

Front Assembly Diagram

Red arrow indicates cast-on edge for each block.

Socks

Socks

Socks

Socks

Socks

Socks

Socks

Crew Socks

Cuff

Loosely CO 40 (48, 56) sts. Arrange evenly on three needles and join into a circle, being careful not to twist your sts.

Next round: *K1, P1, repeat from * to end or round.

Repeat this round until piece measures 1" from beg.

Leg

Next round: * K3, P1, repeat from * to end of round.

Repeat this round until piece measures 3" (3¾", 4½") from beg.

Divide for Heel

K9 (11, 13), m1. Sl remaining sts on this needle to needle 2 for holding. Turn work. sl 1, P19 (23, 27). Move remaining sts on this needle to needle 2 for holding. You now have 21 (25, 29) sts held on needle 2 for your instep, and 20 (24, 28) sts to work for your heel flap.

Heel Flap (worked back and forth in rows)

Row 1 (RS): * Sl 1, K1, repeat from * to end of row.
Row 2: Sl 1, P to end of row.

Repeat these two rows 9 (11, 13) times more, then work row 1 again—21 (25, 29) rows.

Turn Heel

Row 1 (WS): Sl 1, P10 (12, 14), P2tog, P1, turn.
Row 2: Sl 1, K3, K2tog, K1, turn.
Row 3: Sl 1, P4, P2tog, P1, turn.
Row 4: Sl 1, K5, Kk2tog, K1, turn.
Row 5: Sl 1, P6, P2tog, P1, turn.
Row 6: Sl 1, K7, K2tog, K1, turn.
Row 7: Sl 1, P8, P2tog, P1, turn.
Row 8: Sl 1, K9, K2tog, K1.

For first size, 12 sts remain—proceed to *Pick up Sts for Gussets*. For second and third sizes, continue as follows:

Row 9: Sl 1, P10, P2tog, P1, turn.
Row 10: Sl 1, K11, K2tog, K1.

For second size, 14 sts remain—proceed to *Pick up Sts for Gussets*. For third size, continue as follows:

Row 11: Sl 1, P12, P2tog, P1, turn.
Row 12: Sl 1, K13, K2tog, K1—16 sts remain.

Pick up Sts for Gussets

Continuing with the needle holding your heel sts, pick up and knit 10 (12, 14) sts down the left side of heel flap. Using a second needle, work 21 (25, 29) sts at instep in rib pattern as established. Using a third

These classic crew socks will be worn every day.
The ribbed leg helps the socks stay up.

needle, pick up and knit 10 (12, 14) stitches up the right side of heel flap. K6 (7, 8) sts to center of heel—53 (63, 73) sts. Beg of round is at center of heel. K one round.

Decrease Gussets
Round 1:
Needle 1—K to last 3 sts, K2tog, K1.
Needle 2—Work in rib pattern as established.
Needle 3—K1, SSK, K to end of round.
Round 2:
Needle 1—K.
Needle 2—Work in rib pattern as established.
Needle 3—K.

Alternate these two rounds 5 (6, 7) times more—41 (49, 57) sts.

Foot
Continue without shaping until foot measures 3½" (4¼", 5¼") from back of heel (or desired length to base of big toe). On final round, dec 1 st at center of needle 2—40 (48, 56) sts.

Shape Toe
Round 1:
Needle 1—K to last 3 sts, K2tog, K1.
Needle 2—K1, SSK, K to last 3 sts, K2tog, K1.
Needle 3—K1, SSK, K to end of round.
Round 2: K.

Repeat these 2 rounds 3 (4, 5) times more—24 (28, 32) sts. Discontinue round 2 and dec as for round 1 on every round until 8 sts remain. Break yarn and draw through remaining sts. Pull tight, and fasten off.

Wavy Rib Pattern (multiple of 6)
Rounds 1 & 2: * K3, P3, repeat from * to end of round.
Rounds 3 & 4: K2, * P3, K3, repeat from * to last 4 sts, end with P3, K1.
Rounds 5 & 6: K1, * P3, K3, repeat from * to last 5 sts, end with P3, K2.
Rounds 7 & 8: * P3, K3, repeat from * to end of round.
Rounds 9 & 10: Repeat Rounds 5 & 6.
Rounds 11 & 12: Repeat Rounds 3 & 4.

Repeat these 12 rounds for pattern.

Leg
Loosely CO 54 (60, 66) sts. Divide evenly on three needles and join into a circle, being careful not to twist your sts. Work in Wavy Rib Pattern for 9" (11", 13").

Shape Toe
Round 1: K.
Round 2: * K4, K2tog, repeat from * to end of round.
Rounds 3-6: K.
Round 7: * K3, K2tog, repeat from * to end of round.
Rounds 8-10: K.
Round 11: * K2, K2tog, repeat from * to end of round.
Rounds 12 & 13: K.
Round 14: * K1, K2tog, repeat from * to end of round.
Round 15: K.
Round 16: K2tog 9 (10, 11) times.
Round 17: K2tog 3 (5, 4) times, K3tog 1 (0, 1) time.

Break yarn and draw through remaining sts. Pull tight, and fasten off.

DIFFICULTY INTERMEDIATE

YARN LANA GROSSA MEILENWEIT MAGICO (100 (100, 100) GRAMS)

NEEDLES SET OF FOUR DOUBLE-POINTED US 1 (2.25 MM) *OR THE SIZE YOU NEED TO GET GAUGE*

SIZES SHOE SIZE 4-5 (6-8, 9-12)

GAUGE 32 STS AND 40 ROWS = 4" IN STOCKINETTE STITCH

Tube Socks

When their feet seem to grow longer by the day, try tube socks. Because the heel is not defined, the fit is much more forgiving.

YARN LANA GROSSA MEILENWEIT INCA (100 (100, 100) GRAMS)

NEEDLES SET OF FOUR DOUBLE-POINTED US 1 (2.25 MM)
OR THE SIZE YOU NEED TO GET GAUGE

SIZES SHOE SIZE 4-5 (6-8, 9-12)

GAUGE 32 STS AND 40 ROWS = 4" IN STOCKINETTE STITCH

Knee Socks

*Knee socks are a wardrobe
essential for every girl.
This pair will add a shot of
bright color to her
skirts and shorts. The wide
ribbing pattern helps
the socks contour to
the shape of her leg.*

Cuff

Loosely CO 42 (48, 54) sts. Arrange evenly on three needles and join into a circle, being careful not to twist your sts.

Next round: *K1, P1, repeat from * to end of round.

Repeat this round until piece measures 1" from beg.

Leg

Next round: * K5, P1, repeat from * to end of round.

Repeat this round until piece measures 8" (9", 10") from beg.

Divide for Heel

K9 (11, 13), m1. Slip remaining sts on this needle to needle 2 for holding. Turn work. sl 1, P19 (23, 27). Move remaining sts on this needle to needle 2 for holding. You now have 23 (25, 27) sts held on needle 2 for your instep, and 20 (24, 28) sts to work for your heel flap.

Heel Flap (worked back and forth in rows)

Row 1 (RS): * Sl 1, K1, repeat from * to end of row.
Row 2: Sl 1, P to end of row.

Repeat these two rows 9 (11, 13) times more, then work row 1 again—21 (25, 29) rows.

Turn Heel

Row 1 (WS): Sl 1, P10 (12, 14), P2tog, P1, turn.
Row 2: Sl 1, K3, K2tog, K1, turn.
Row 3: Sl 1, P4, P2tog, P1, turn.
Row 4: Sl 1, K5, K2tog, K1, turn.
Row 5: Sl 1, P6, P2tog, P1, turn.
Row 6: Sl 1, K7, K2tog, K1, turn.
Row 7: Sl 1, P8, P2tog, P1, turn.
Row 8: Sl 1, K9, K2tog, K1.

For first size, 12 sts remain—proceed to *Pick up Sts for Gussets*. For second and third sizes, continue as follows:

Row 9: Sl 1, P10, P2tog, P1, turn.
Row 10: Sl 1, K11, K2tog, K1.

For second size, 14 sts remain—proceed to *Pick up Sts for Gussets*. For third size, continue as follows:

Row 11: Sl 1, P12, P2tog, P1, turn.
Row 12: Sl 1, K13, K2tog, k1—16 sts remain.

Pick up Sts for Gussets

Continuing with the needle holding your heel sts, pick up and knit 10 (12, 14) sts down the left side of heel flap. Using a second needle, work 23 (25, 27) sts at instep in rib pattern as established. Using a third needle, pick up and knit 10 (12, 14) stitches up the right side of heel flap. K6 (7, 8) sts to center of heel—55 (63, 71) sts. Beg of round is at center of heel. K one round.

Decrease Gussets

Round 1:
Needle 1—K to last 3 sts, K2tog, K1.
Needle 2—Work in rib pattern as established.
Needle 3—K1, SSK, K to end of round.
Round 2:
Needle —K.
Needle 2—Work in rib pattern as established.
Needle 3—K.

Alternate these two rounds 5 (6, 7) times more—43 (49, 55) sts.

Foot

Continue without shaping until foot measures 3½" (4¼", 5¼") from back of heel (or desired length to base of big toe). On final round, dec 1 st at center of needle 2—42 (48, 54) sts.

Shape Toe

Round 1:
Needle 1—K to last 3 sts, K2tog, K1.
Needle 2—K1, SSK, K to last 3 sts, K2tog, K1.
Needle 3—K1, SSK, K to end of round.
Round 2: K.

Repeat these 2 rounds 3 (4, 5) times more—26 (28, 30) sts.

Discontinue round 2 and dec as for round 1 on every round until 6 (8, 6) sts remain. Break yarn and draw through remaining sts. Pull tight, and fasten off.

Nap Time

Nap Time

Nap Time

Nap Time

Nap Time

Nap Blanket

Cozy and warm, this is the blanket your child will want to carry everywhere. The entrelac technique gives it the look of intricate patchwork.

DIFFICULTY INTERMEDIATE

YARN LANA GROSSA MEILENWEIT INCA (300 GRAMS)

NEEDLES TWO 24" CIRCULAR AND 1 DOUBLE-POINTED US 2 (2.75 MM) *OR THE SIZE YOU NEED TO GET GAUGE.*

MEASUREMENTS 24" X 30", NOT INCLUDING BORDER

GAUGE 12 STS AND 24 ROWS = 2" IN GARTER STITCH

Notes

◆ This body of this blanket is 12 blocks wide by 15 blocks long. Knit the body in one piece using the entrelac technique, working on one set of needles from block to block without breaking yarn in diagonal tiers (composed of a series of blocks) from one corner of blanket to the opposite corner, joining tiers together as you work. See schematic on page 70.

◆ To knit the border, first pick up sts along the edge of blanket, then attach border to these stitches as you knit it.

◆ Use the **Cable Cast-On Method** throughout as follows: Make a slip knot and place on left-hand needle. Insert right-hand needle through loop as if to knit, wrap yarn around right-hand needle and pull loop through, twist, and place on left-hand needle. *Insert right-hand needle between 1st and 2nd sts on left-hand needle, wrap yarn around right-hand needle and pull loop through, twist, and place on left-hand needle; rep from *.

◆ Slip sts at beg of rows as if to purl with yarn in front.

Blanket

Blocks A–I are defined on page 71.

Tier 1: Work Block A.

Tier 2: Work Block B, then Block C.

Tier 3: Work Block B, then Block D, then Block E.

Tier 4: Work Block B, then Block F 2 times, then Block C.

Tier 5: Work Block B, then Block D 3 times, then Block E.

Tier 6: Work Block B, then Block F 4 times, then Block C.

Tier 7: Work Block B, then Block D 5 times, then Block E.

Tier 8: Work Block B, then Block F 6 times, then Block C.

Tier 9: Work Block B, then Block D 7 times, then Block E.

Tier 10: Work Block B, then Block F 8 times, then Block C.

Tier 11: Work Block B, then Block D 9 times, then Block E.

Tier 12: Work Block B, then Block F 10 times, then Block C. BO 11 sts.

Tier 13: Work Block G, then Block D 10 times, then Block E.

Tier 14: Work Block B, then Block F 11 times. BO 11 sts.

Tier 15: Work Block G, then Block D 10 times, then Block H.

Tier 16: Work Block I, then Block F 10 times. BO 11 sts.

Tier 17: Work Block G, then Block D 8 times, then Block H.

Tier 18: Work Block I, then Block F 8 times. BO 11 sts.

Tier 19: Work Block G, then Block D 6 times, then Block H.

Tier 20: Work Block I, then Block F 6 times. BO 11 sts.

Tier 21: Work Block G, then Block D 4 times, then Block H.

Tier 22: Work Block I, then Block F 4 times. BO 11 sts.

Tier 23: Work Block G, then Block D 2 times, then Block H.

Tier 24: Work Block I, then Block F 2 times. BO 11 sts.

Tier 25: Work Block G, then Block H.

Tier 26: Work Block I. BO all sts.

Border

Using circular needle, RS facing, pick up and knit 12 sts at the side of each block all the way around the blanket—648 sts (you will need to use both of your circular needles to hold all these sts).

CO 3 sts. Use the double-pointed needle to hold your border sts (the left-hand needle on RS rows).

Set-up row (WS): K2, K2tog (last st of border with 1 st picked up at edge of blanket).

Row 1 (RS): Sl 1, K1, m1, K1.

Row 2: Sl 1, K2, K2tog (last st of border with 1 st picked up at edge of blanket).

Row 3: Sl 1, K2, m1, K1.

Row 4: Sl 1, K3, K2tog (last st of border with 1 st picked up at edge of blanket).

Row 5: Sl 1, K3, m1, K1.

Row 6: Sl 1, K4, K2tog (last st of border with 1 st picked up at edge of blanket).

Row 7: Sl 1, K4, m1, K1.

Row 8: Sl 1, K5, K2tog (last st of border with 1 st picked up at edge of blanket).

Row 9: Sl 1, K5, m1, K1.

Row 10: Sl 1, K6, K2tog (last st of border with 1 st picked up at edge of blanket).

Row 11: Sl 1, K6, m1, K1.

Row 12: Sl 1, K7, K2tog (last st of border with 1 st picked up at edge of blanket).

Row 13: Sl 1, K5, K2tog, K1.

Row 14: Sl 1, K6, K2tog (last st of border with 1 st picked up at edge of blanket).

Row 15: Sl 1, K4, K2tog, K1.

Row 16: Sl 1, K5, K2tog (last st of border with 1 st picked up at edge of blanket).

Row 17: Sl 1, K3, K2tog, K1.

Row 18: Sl 1, K4, K2tog (last st of border with 1 st picked up at edge of blanket).

Row 19: Sl 1, K2, K2tog, K1.

Row 20: Sl 1, K3, K2tog (last st of border with 1 st picked up at edge of blanket).

Row 21: Sl 1, K1, K2tog, K1.

Row 22: Sl 1, K2, K2tog (last st of border with 1 st picked up at edge of blanket).

Row 23: Sl 1, K2tog, K1.

Row 24: Sl 1, K1, K2tog (last st of border with 1 st picked up at edge of blanket).

Repeat these 24 rows 53 times more. BO.

Finishing

Sew beg and end of border together. Weave in ends. Block to finished measurements.

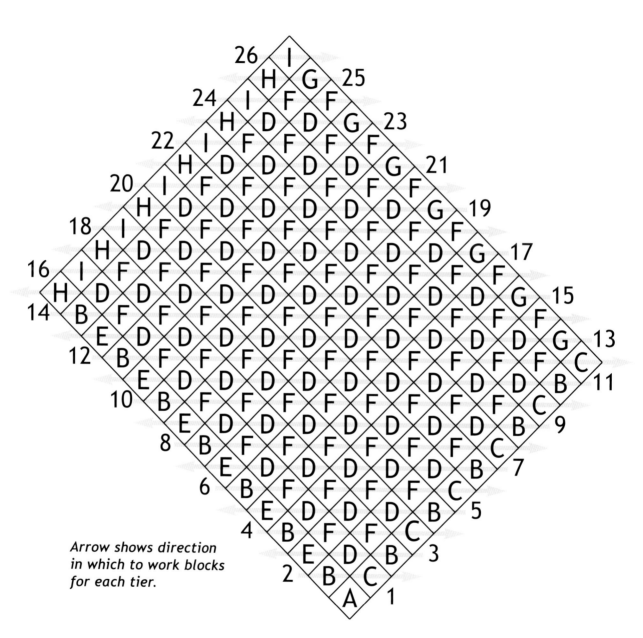

Arrow shows direction
in which to work blocks
for each tier.

Blocks

Block A: CO 12 sts.

Rows 1-24: Sl 1, K11.

Block B: CO 12 sts.

Row 1: Sl 1, K10, K2tog (last st of this block with one st from adjoining block).
Row 2: Sl 1, K11.

Repeat these 2 rows 10 times more, then work row 1 again.

Block C: Pick up and purl 12 sts down side of adjoining block.

Rows 1-24: Sl 1, K11.

Block D: Pick up and knit 12 sts down side of adjoining block.

Row 1: Sl 1, K11.
Row 2: Sl 1, K10, K2tog (last st of this block with one st from the adjoining block).

Repeat these 2 rows 11 times more.

Block E: Pick up and knit 12 sts down side of adjoining block.

Rows 1-24: Sl 1, K11.

Block F: Pick up and purl 12 sts down side of adjoining block.

Row 1: Sl 1, K11.
Row 2: Sl 1, K10, K2tog (last st of this block with one st from adjoining block).

Repeat these 2 rows 11 times more.

Block G: Pick up and knit 11 sts down side of adjoining block.

Row 1: Sl 1, K11.
Row 2: Sl 1, K10, K2tog (last st of this block with one st from the adjoining block).

Repeat these 2 rows 11 times more.

Block H: Pick up and knit 12 sts down side of adjoining block.

Rows 1-23: Sl 1, K11.
BO 11 sts—1 st remains.

Block I: Pick up and purl 11 sts down side of last block worked.

Row 1: Sl 1, K11.
Row 2: Sl 1, K10, K2tog (last st of this block with one st from the adjoining block).

Repeat these 2 rows 11 times more.

Lana Grossa Meilenweit Sock Yarn
Yarn Styles and Colors Used

Project	Shown on Page	Yarn Style/Color
Cabled Vest	21, 22	Mega Boots Stretch/707
Cape	4, 19, 24, 27	Meeting/7760
Crew Socks	59	Colortweed/1003
Dancer's Wrap	45, 47	Multieffekt/3122
Elfin Hat	3, 17	Multiringel/5124
Girl's Jumper	29, 30, Back Cover	Multiringel/5020
Hooded Pullover	Front Cover, 7, 40	Magico/2528
Knee Socks	63, 64	Inca/1527
Leg Warmers	45, 47, 48	Multieffekt/3122
Nap Blanket	67, 72	Inca/1531
Patchwork Pullover	39, 51, 52	Fantasy/4837
Ruffled Mittens	34	Colortweed/1001
Swirly Hat	11, 12, Back Cover	Magico/2525
Tube Socks	57, 60, 61	Magico/2521
X-Ribbed Mittens	33, 36, 75, Back Cover	Meeting/7730
Wormy Hat	15	Fantasy/4730

Lana Grossa Meilenweit sock yarns are available at fine knitting stores.

For a store near you, call Unicorn Books and Crafts at 1-800-289-9276.

Abbreviations

beg—beginning

BO—bind off

CO—cast on

dec—decrease

dbl dec (double decrease)—sl 2 sts together as if to knit them together, k1, pass 2 slipped sts over the knit stitch.

garter stitch—when working in rows, knit every row; when working in rounds, alternate knit and purl rounds.

inc—increase

K—knit

K2tog—knit 2 stitches together

K3tog—knit 3 stitches together

knitted cord—with 4 sts on needle, K4, *do not turn; push sts to opposite end of needle, bring yarn across back of stitches and K4; rep from * until desired length.

m1 (make 1)—use the tip of your left needle to lift up the strand running between the stitch just worked and the next stitch; knit into the back of this strand, twisting the loop to avoid making a hole.

pm—place marker

P—purl

psso—pass the slipped stitch over the st just knitted

P2tog—purl 2 stitches together

RS—right side

sl—slip

SSK (slip, slip, knit)—slip 1 st as if to knit; slip another st as if to knit; slip both sts back to left-hand needle and knit them together through back loop.

st st (stockinette stitch)—when working in rows, knit the right side rows and purl the wrong side rows; when working in the round, knit every round.

st(s)—stitch(es)

W&T (wrap and turn)—Used to prevent holes at the turning point in short rows. With yarn in back, sl next st to right-hand needle, bring yarn to front, sl st back to left-hand needle and turn the piece, ready to work back in the other direction.

WS—wrong side

yo (inc)—yarn over needle

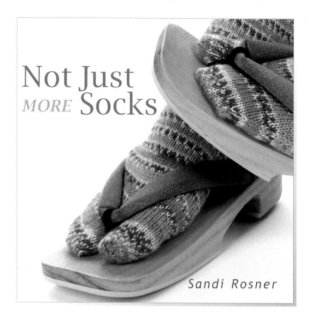

Not Just Socks for Kids is the third installment in **SANDI ROSNER's** popular self-striping sock yarn series. Her first two books, **Not Just Socks** and **Not Just More Socks**, continue to be best sellers. In this new volume, Sandi explores the possibilities of using colorful Lana Grossa sock yarn for children's clothes that are both fun to knit and practical to wear. Much in demand as a designer and teacher, Sandi's work can be seen in many knitting magazines and books. When in Sebastopol, California, be sure to visit her store, Knitting Workshop.